Old Stones of the Cotswolds
& Forest of Dean

A survey of megaliths and mark stones past and present
by
D.P. Sullivan

The Tibblestone

Reardon Publishing

Published
by
REARDON PUBLISHING
56 Upper Norwood Street,
Cheltenham, Glos, GL53 0DU.
www.reardon.co.uk

Reardon Publishing
Copyright ©1999

Reardon & Son
Old Stones of Gloucestershire
ISBN 1-873877-00-5
Copyright ©1991

Original text and Photographs
except where otherwise credited
D.P. SULLIVAN

ISBN 1-873877-37-4

Cover Design
Nicholas Reardon

Book Design and Layout
Peter T Reardon

Drawings & illustrations
Peter T Reardon

Cover Photographs
Copyright © Nicholas Reardon
Inset stone "The Tibblestone"

Printed by
In2Print
Cheltenham

AUTHOR'S NOTE

This guide to the old stone monuments of Gloucestershire is derived from a series of articles which first appeared in **Gloucestershire Earth Mysteries** magazine between 1987 and 1990. The list of sites is constantly being added to via information passed on by correspondents and by chance encounters in the field. The following guide is designed for the curious, the megalith hunter, walker and antiquary alike. It does not profess to being exhaustive, but it is my intention to keep the survey up to date and any additions to it will appear in subsequent editions of the above publication. I would be pleased to hear from any reader of this work who has knowledge of the whereabouts of other stones not included here, or of legends, stories, anecdotes, old drawings, or photographs relating to those which are.

I would like to thank the following people who knowingly or unknowingly have helped me in the compilation of this survey; Anne Hewitt, Louise King, The Stanley Partnership, Alan Lovejoy, David James, Roger Cudby, Bob Trubshaw, Ray Wright, Ron Fletcher, Tim Holland Chris Hall and O.G.S. Crawford.

Gloucestershire Earth Mysteries is available, by subscription, from The Editor, Gloucestershire Earth Mysteries, P.O. Box 258, Cheltenham, Gloucestershire, GL53 0HR.

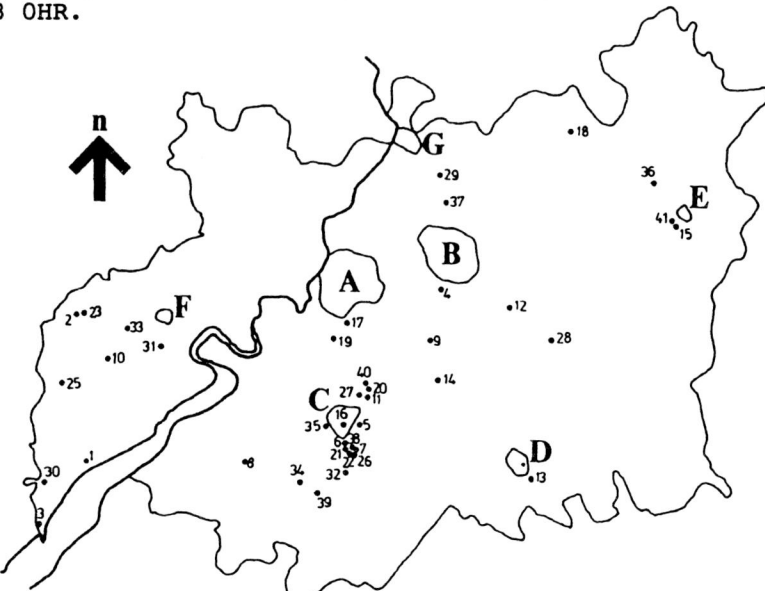

Distribution of sites in the county

KEY: A-Gloucester, B-Cheltenham, C-Stroud, D-Cirencester, E-Stow-on-the-Wold, F-Cinderford, G-Tewkesbury

INTRODUCTION

A glance at the Ordnance Survey or any guide to prehistoric sites in England will reveal little in the way of ancient stones in Gloucestershire. The county can boast a considerable number of long barrows whose megaliths remain largely buried, but no stone circles and, apparently, few standing stones. The reality, however, is a legacy of many monoliths, lost megaliths, forgotten mark stones, boundary stones, once venerated natural rocks and ancient milestones scattered all over the county.

In the research for this survey an invaluable source of information has been O G S Crawford's **Long Barrows of the Cotswolds**, published in the late 1920s, which lists many sites, both natural and man-made. Crawford's interest in long barrows led him to conclude that most standing stones were either remains of the chambers of denuded barrows, or, at best, natural boulders, or recent erections. In some cases it is now accepted that certain prehistoric standing stones were unlikely to have been part of a long barrow and that they were erected for some, now, unknown purpose.

Alfred Watkins of Hereford, in the 1920s, postulated that single standing stones were erected to mark 'the old straight track', prehistoric trading routes which made their way in dead straight lines across country, linking prominent topographical features. He coined the term **ley** to describe these ancient alignments. The full account of his discovery and theories can be found in his book **The Old Straight Track**. Mark stones were placed along the track to guide the traveller and were often placed at the crossing point of two leys. An important stone in the Forest of Dean, in the parish of Staunton, is the Long Stone. This is located at the crossing point of two major alignments of ancient sites, running north-south and east-west. A description of 'The Leyline Cross', is given by its discoverer, Ray Wright, in his book **Secret Forest**.

Much recent thinking into the ley hypothesis has linked ancient standing stones to a form of terrestrial energy. Dowsers, water diviners and certain sensitive people claim to be able to detect this energy which is prominent at certain specific locations. This detectable effect is probably electromagnetic in origin. and it has been suggested that prehistoric man was aware of these forces and marked their location with sacred structures such as stone circles and standing stones. In this way these special places could always be recognised and readily located.

A research project was set up some ten years ago to investigate scientifically whether the 'energies', believed by dowsers and fringe antiquarians alike to be present at ancient sacred sites, had any basis in reality. This investigation was the Dragon Project and its tentative conclusions can be found in Paul Devereux's **Places of Power**, the first attempt to frame the findings of the Project in a theoretical context. Devereux suggests that sacred places may have been selected or sited by prehistoric peoples in order to utilise specific environmental effects to enhance magical, shamanistic and other activities and rituals that took place there. He shows that many ancient sacred sites are associated with anomalous geophysical effects such as strange lights, paranormal events and electromagnetic energy effects. Similar effects, in relation to some of the Gloucestershire stones, are described in the following survey.

The record of folklore, anecdotal evidence for anomalous phenomena and the body of evidence from dowsers and psychics, who claim to have detected energy effects at ancient sites, suggests that our ancestors may have developed a technology whereby their shamans, priests or holy men could interact with the spirit world through altered states of consciousness brought about by contact with localised electromagnetic energy fields. Such fields occur naturally at venerated spots and were marked, and possibly enhanced, by the erection of megalithic structures such as stone circles and standing stones.

It is notoriously difficult to date the erection of a standing stone, but most are believed to have been erected in the Bronze Age (c1500BC). Some may be earlier. The standing stones in the following survey are not all prehistoric and certainly not all contemporaneous. Some have been erected for quite mundane purposes, to mark the way, to commemorate a battle, to define a boundary. Others have no obvious significance and seem to have been put up for some esoteric reasons that we may never fully understand.

THE BROADSTONE (No.1)
Parish of Tidenham
ST 57769723

This monolith consists of Lias limestone which has some imbedded quartz pebbles and lies just above the high water mark between the railway and the A48 Gloucester to Chepstow road, near the boundary between Tidenham and Woolaston at a place called Stroat. The Broadstone stands eight and a half feet high, one and a quarter feet thick and five and a half feet wide at the base (2.6m x 0.69m x 1.68m). I tapers to a point. The Archaeological Record suggests that its position on the Severn alluvium is unusual (for a standing stone) and that it may well have marked a crossing at this point. Crawford quotes a correspondent, Mr A.E.W. Paine of Cheltenham, "There is the usual local tradition that (the Broadstone) was thrown by the Devil – in this case the tale being that it was thrown from Tidenham Chace (sic) at Thornbury Church on the other side of the river, and fell short". Ray Wright elaborates on this story. The Devil and Jack o' Kent tried their strength in a stone throwing contest. The Devil threw first and heaved the Broadstone to where it now stands, but Jack won the contest as he managed to heave his stone right across the Severn to Thornbury. Wright suggests that 'Jack's pebble', from a traditional verse may well have been a stone that was once purported to have stood between Oldbury and a village near Thornbury called Stone. The modern Ordnance Survey map offers no clues as to its whereabouts. Is it still there?

Mr J.G. Wood, quoted by Crawford, says,

"There are several other stones near marked on the 6-inch map between the railway and the Roman road. None are boundary stones; but I believe they are all 'drifters'". In **Secret Forest** Ray Wright mentions an ancient trackway which runs westwards by the north side of Stroat House, on the A48. On the opposite side of the road it continues past Stroat Farm to Tidenham Chase. On its bank lies a row of upright stones. These are mentioned in the Tidenham Saxon Charter as part of the boundary of the manor.

It has been noticed by leyhunters that such stories of giants or the Devil throwing a stone from a prominent hilltop can sometimes reflect a folk memory of the marking of an alignment in the distant past. At present there is insufficient information from which to draw any conclusions. Locating Jack's pebble might give some clues.

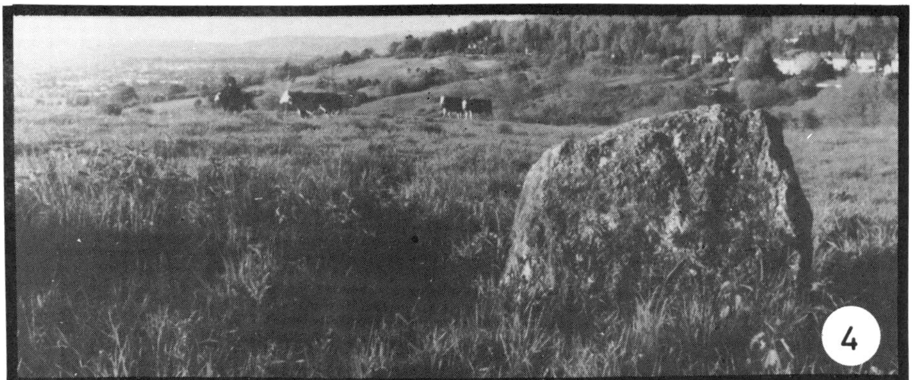
4

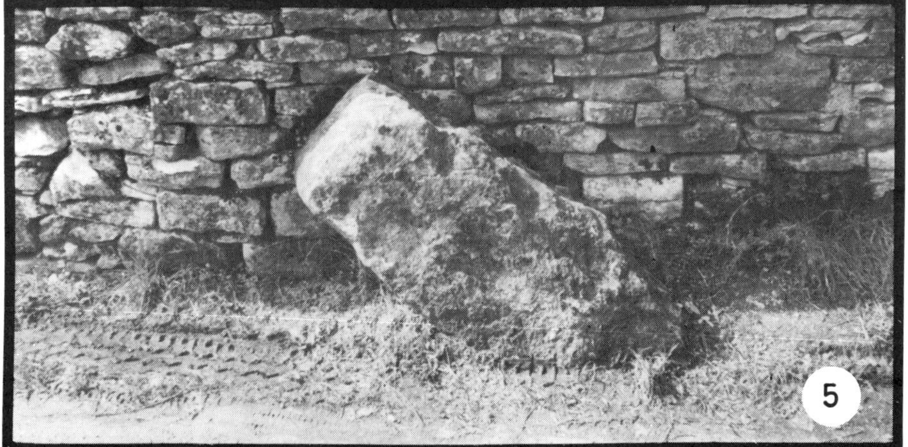
5

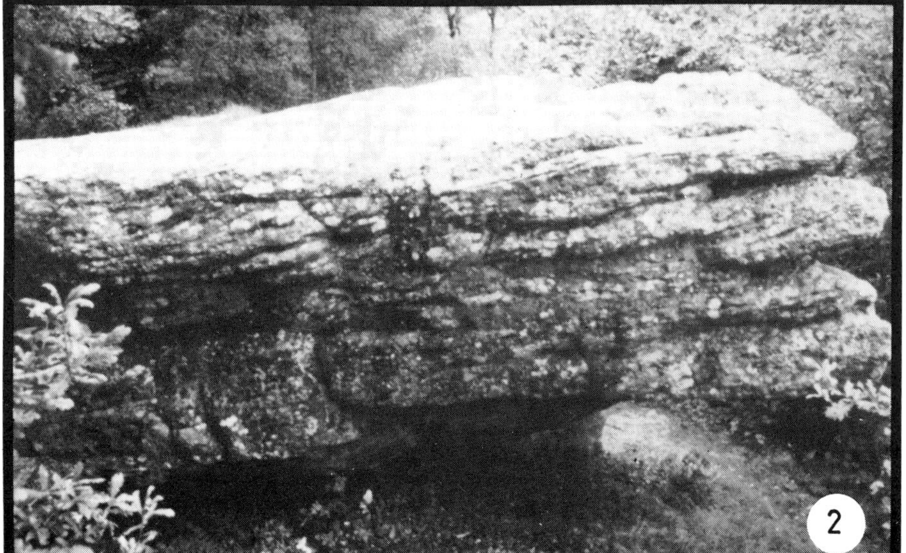
2

THE BUCKSTONE (No.2)
Parish of Staunton
SO 54151230

A description of this natural rock was mentioned by Louis Jennings in **Field and Green Lanes** in 1878:

"In the south-east, that curious rocking stone, the Buckstone, can be discerned, and there is a path from the Kymin to it, chiefly through woods or across fields. The site of the Buckstone is marked by a small flagstaff, a stone weighing hundreds of tons, yet poised upon a piece of rock scarcely two feet broad, like a huge top standing upon its peg. The hill runs down a thousand feet sheer below it, and the stone inclines over at an acute angle, and can be rocked by a strong man. An old fellow, whom I overtook on the common, told me that the frolicsome youth of Staunton had one night come up here armed with 'picks' and crowbars, but could not move it. "It is considered", this old man said to me, "as it was washed there when the world was drowned".

Just beyond the centre of Staunton on the A4136 Monmouth road is a narrow lane on the left. This works its way up the hill and to a trackway which climbs to the trigonometrical pillar at 279 metres, close by an underground reservoir. Below the pillar the ground falls away dramatically offering extensive views across the Wye and into Wales. Immediately below the edge lies the Buckstone, a natural pyramidal mass of quartz conglomerate, seemingly perched on its inverted apex. It was, at one time, believed to have been a rocking or 'logan' stone, 'placed in its present position by Druidical agency', and that it was possible, with apparent ease, to push the massive boulder to and fro on its point. The continuing onslaught of the elements, which fashioned this curiosity out of the softer surrounding strata, eventually wore away at the pivot preventing further rocking of the Buckstone. Various attempts, over the years, to get the stone to move resulted in its being dislodged in 1885. It toppled over, breaking into several pieces. Local worthies set about restoring the Buckstone and it was reconstituted and set back on its pivot by the insertion of a steel reinforcing rod. Further movement of the stone has been permanently arrested.

Immediately west of the Buckstone and on a lower level is Broadstones Farm, taking its name from a set of broad stones between the road and the line of the Roman road just north of the farm. They are all of Old Red Conglomerate.

BUTTINGTON TUMP (No.3)
Parish of Tidenham
ST 54789306

Crawford quotes Mr J.G. Wood:

"On Buttington Tump (part of Offa's Dyke) is an erect stone, bedded in others and marked as 'standing stone'. It may be as old as the dyke but not older; and I have a suspicion that its erection is somewhat modern, and that it was put there when the road to Beachley was improved and the hill cut down. It was possibly found to be in the way".

The Archaeological Record mentions road widening in 1960 which cut into the dyke. A rescue operation revealed an erect stone, four and a half feet (1.37m) high, on the highest point of the tump resting on a circular base of four flat irregular slabs, all of local sandstone. It was believed to be the 'handiwork of an antiquarian landowner'. The stones were re-erected 25ft (7.62m) west of their original position. The upright stone might be the remains of Sedbury Cross, moved itself from its former site. A well travelled stone.

Ray Wright, in **Secret Forest** mentions Buttinghton or Ormerod's Stone which he reports was erected during the 19th Century by Dr George Ormerod to mark the spot where King Alfred is said to have defeated the Danes. The stone was pushed over one night by vandals and now lies in the brambles. Wright suggests that the name Buttington comes from **butt**, an early meaning of which was **stone**. From this he implies that Buttington Tump could have meant a bank with a stone and, further that Dr Ormerod may have re-erected an existing stone or replaced it with a new one.

BLACK HEDGE FARM STONE CIRCLES (No.4)
Parish of Leckhampton

In 1986 whilst idly perusing a 1950's edition of Johnston's coloured touring map of Gloucestershire I was intrigued to spot an antiquity marked south-west of Leckhampton Hill as 'stone circles'. However, upon scrutinising the modern Ordnance Survey maps no trace of this site could be found. The Parish Records of Leckhampton carry an article from the parish magazine for 1897 by R.C. Barnard:

"...these curious stones on Black Hedge Farm, which the Ordnance Survey has adopted as real antiquities, and are called 'Stone Circles'. I don't know exactly what I think on the subject. I find that I am disposed to deny or defend their genuine antiquity, according as the person I am with is inclined to defend or deny it. There is plenty to say on either side of the question. The stones may possibly have fallen from the cliffs above into their present position. On the other hand, some of them seem to have been placed by human hands, but there are not more than one or two of which I think that can be said positively".

I have visited the site. There are what appear to be three distinct groups of megaliths; two groups scattered amidst dilapidated earthworks and a group of stones approximately three feet high. On a subsequent visit further stones were located in the undergrowth beyond the drystone wall, below the escarpment. The fields around the site are dotted with six springs and a well. Above on the higher ground, not far away, lies the ancient trackway called the Greenway, the Crippets or Shurdington long barrow on Barrow Piece and a ruined round barrow. Curiously the major stones, which are still visible (some are recumbent and some partially buried) are of classic 'holey stone' and must have been exposed to the elements for many centuries.

Mr Barnard may have been indecisive but Mr Crawford harbours no reservations. He was convinced that they were "without the least doubt of recent origin". He goes on to explain how they were probably pushed to the edge of the field to facilitate cultivation. One must assume he means the field above the escarpment. He later concedes that,

"it is possible, with the aid of a strong imagination and no plan, to look on them as remains of a disturbed stone circle"

The present site of the stones, at the foot of an escarpment, is not a classic stone circle site as the scarp blocks off any view to the south. if anything the stones have probably been pushed from the field above. That site is far more promising as a site for a circle or group of stones.

Blackhedge Farm is private property and permission should be sought from the owner if you wish to visit the site. The stones can be seen from the path that leads from the old quarry close to Blackhedge Farm leading up to the hillfort on Leckhampton Hill.

STONE AT CHALFORD (No.5)
On the Chalford-Hyde-Minchinhampton road

This unworked stone is mentioned in **Milestones of the Stroud District**, by Christopher Cox, from the **Transactions of the Bristol and Gloucestershire Archaeological Society**:

"At the foot of the hill just before the road turns to avoid the canal on the left against the wall is a stone of the general shape of a milestone, measuring 17ins by 10ins by 36ins. It has no discernable remains of letters, nor signs of having had a plate. However, neither does it have any indication of former use as a gatepost and there is no companion on the other side of the road. Rather tentatively, it is put here as a possible milestone, though the distance from the Hyde stone is less than a mile; but of course that stone may not have been one of a series."

The stone is still insitu, although leaning over, lying beside the wall to the Belvedere millpond.

THE COBSTONE (No.6)
Parish of Minchinhampton
Lost. ST856000 or ST 877899 (site of)

This "remarkably fine stone" once occupied a spot on the edge of Minchinhampton Common due west of the Long Stone and due north of the Peaked Stone (No.32), although its exact location is not known. It was removed in about 1836 and used for building materials.

THE DEVIL'S CHURCHYARD (No.7)
Parish of Minchinhampton
SO 899003

The Devil's Churchyard is situated east of Minchinhampton between Crackstone and Dunkerpool. Roughly equidistant from it are, in the north-east, a circular depression which may have been used for ritual purposes; in the south-east, at Aston, an early enclosure; in the south-west, the Long Stone; and in the west, a now destroyed long barrow at Crackstone. It is a roughly L-shaped enclosure in open cultivated fields which comprise part of the Gatcombe Park estate. As with the Tinglestone access should only be made with the permission of the landowner.

There were once large stones in the Devil's Churchyard which may have been connected with the Old Religion, practised before the advent of Christianity. In opposition to this when the incumbent of the Lammas, in Minchinhampton, decided that a new church should be built he chose to site it in the place of pagan worship, as was the approved practice. However, no sooner had the work commenced than it was mysteriously torn down in the night. Eventually the work was abandoned, the vandalism being attributed to the Devil. The standing stones were subsequently removed, at the instigation of the former incumbent, being accounted unholy, having supposedly been used for Devil worship and sacrificial purposes. The church was instead built on its present site in Minchinhampton and the Lammas stones faded into obscurity. All that remains on site are tales of eerie noises being heard. In an article in **Gloucestershire Earth Mysteries**, No.3 David James recounts the legend of a ghostly horse and rider which has been seen along the lane which runs past the Devil's Churchyard. When it reaches the site the apparition is said to disappear.

The Gloucestershire Archaeological Records say that it is more than likely that the site was in fact a stone circle. I and several other people have made a cursory examination of the site, but although the odd boulder can be found, no trace of a stone circle is now visble. Some of the stones may well be insitu, but buried. Such 'pagan' stones were often broken up or buried by early Christians who associated the old stones with the Old Religion, then equated with the Devil.

Crawford refers to the stones from the Devil's Garden in a quote from the account of the **Proceedings of the Bristol and Gloucestershire Archaeological Society** at Stroud, July 1880:

"A visit was then made to the yard of Mr Baynes's house, The Lammas, Minchinhampton, to see some large stones which were, many years ago, removed from Cherrington Common, where they occupied a site known as 'The Devil's Garden'. Mr Baynes described the stones at some length. They were evidently taken from the surface of the rock known as the 'Great Oolite'. The surface of this rock is full of holes and is popularly known as the 'holey stone'. A vote of thanks to Mr Baynes, and a suggestion by a member that the stones should be returned to Cherrington and restored to their original position terminated this part of the programme".

Three stones or parts of stones can today be seen inside the gateway to Lammas House in Minchinhampton. It is worth noting that the garden wall of an adjacent cottage is constructed entirely from blocks of severely weathered 'holey stone'; the remains of further stones perhaps.

As a final footnote David James showed me two immense limestone blocks in the grounds of Lammas House which form a footbridge over a hollow way which runs through the gardens to the Minchinhampton spring. Whether or not these two megaliths have any connection with the Lammas stones or the Devil's Churchyard is open to speculation.

DURSLEY MERE STONE (No.8)
On the boundary of the parishes of Dursley and Cam
ST 78579618

Crawford mentions a sketch given in **Gloucestershire Notes and Queries** of a stone which is inscribed 'PD 1663'. The sketch dates from 1886 and is described as an old boundary stone which marked the limits of the parish of Dursley from Cam. This stone was still believed to have been in existence in 1894. It was situated at the sand-pits, on the road from Dursley to Berkeley, at the corner of a narrow bridle path which leads up to Stinchcombe Hill. Is it still there?

STONES AT ELKSTONE (No.9)
Parishes of Elkstone and Cowley

In the churchyard, in Elkstone, just beyond the entrance gate lie three, or possibly four, fragments of stone; one in particular, the 'holey stone' so often the material of ancient standing stones. These fragments lie in a line alongside the path with no apparent purpose. They may be fragments of a larger stone or stones which have been salvaged and given refuge in the churchyard. Perhaps they were on the site when the church was built. They may even be all that remains of the Elkstone after which the village was named. Another stone, this one carved, and probably Saxon, stands secured to the inside wall of the church tower. It has been speculated that this may be the famed Elkstone.

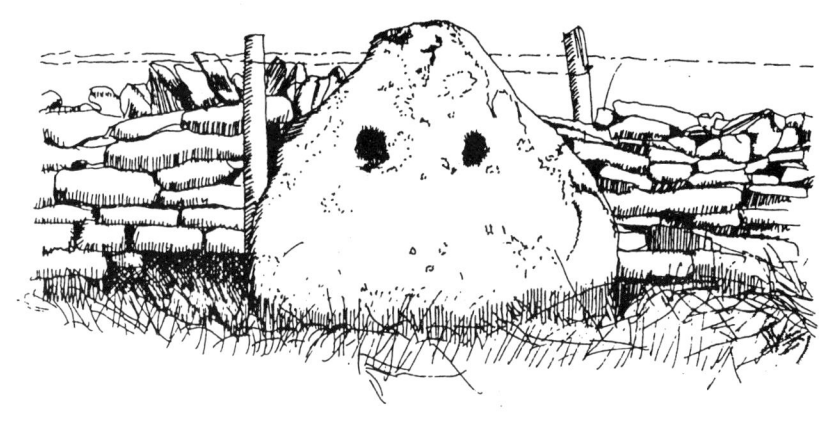

A short distance north of the church is High Cross, the meeting place of four roads. By the side of the road, up against a field wall stands a triangular slab of stone, about 4ft (1.2m) high, 4-5ft (1.2-1.5m) wide, and about a 1ft (0.3m) thick. This is marked on the 1/25000 Ordnance Survey map as a boundary stone. It has two fist sized holes in its face which may have been the fixing points for a metal plate of some kind. However, this is not a milestone. In Cowley Woods below the cross-roads lie several other stones, also marked as boundary stones. These have not been visited by the Author so their existence cannot be verified. The boundary between the parishes defined by these stones is a twisting line, weaving its way through the wood. One could be excused for inferring that the boundary was determined by the locations of the stones rather than vice versa; almost as if these ancient monoliths were adopted as convenient markers to define a later territorial boundary.

Often ancient stones, erected by man in the distant past, were adopted by the Saxons to define a place and its boundaries. For example, in 825 King Egbert granted to the church of St Peter and St Paul at Winchester an estate at Alton, covering the greater part of the present parish. At one point the boundary ran, so the charter tells us, "to a stone in Woncumb in the lower part of (of which) on the upper side is a hole". This stone, a sarsen, with a hole right through it was found by a party working out the bounds of the charter, still where the Saxon 'surveyors' saw it more than eleven centuries ago. (W.G. Hoskins, "The Making of the English Landscape", 1972, p70). This could have been a natural boulder but for the fact of the hole right through it, strongly suggesting that it was a fertility stone and therefore specifically sited in connection with that purpose.

Natural features also made convenient territorial markers. As such, old hundreds were often named after venerated trees, natural and ancient rocks, rivers and lakes, etc. Of course, not all boundary stones are adopted ancient megaliths, but many probably are. So when in search of ancient standing stones do not dismiss boundary stones as unimportant. A visit might confirm their antiquity.

The Archaeological Record records the possible existence of a long barrow site north-west of High Cross as SO 964135. All that remains is an elongated oval scatter of limestone in the cultivated field. A standing stone once stood in the field which may have been a stone from the barrow. This was removed and is believed to be the stone now set by the wall. It was once used as a marker for the Coberley Parish boundary (G.T. Harding, July 1961).

15

GATTLES CROSS (No.10)
Clearwell Meend, Sling
SO 583085

This curious stone monument stands amongst the trees on Clearwell Meend by the side of the B4228 Coleford to Lydney road. It consists of a large square base with a recess in the top surface into which has been inserted an inverted tapering stone. The whole edifice stands at about five feet (1.5m). Ray Wright reports that the shaft was inserted upside down after it had been repeatedly removed by vandals. The cross, which is supposed to have surmounted the top, was probably broken off during one of its withdrawals. According to Wright the Gattles Cross is said to have been placed in this position during the 18th or 19th Century, replacing an older stone reputed to have been erected in 1282 marking the spot where Queen Eleanor rested on her journey from Wales. Indeed the stone was once known as Eleanor's Cross.

A correspondent, Mr Trubshaw, of Leicestershire, wrote to me some years ago:

"Although my visits to Gloucestershire are infrequent, my girlfriend, Ann, and I managed to spend a week in the Forest of Dean during October. Whilst I was attempting to photograph the Gattle Stone an elderly lady came by and started talking to Ann, although I was not in earshot. The essence of the conversation was that she had lived in one of the cottages to the south-east of the stone for much of her life and, about twenty years ago, her husband had seen the ghost of a man dressed in black near to the stone. She said that her husband was a very down-to-earth man, a miner who 'called a shovel an effing spade'. Unfortunately I was not aware of the conversation going on whilst I was otherwise occupied and the lady went away before I rejioned Ann. This account is therefore second-hand and much less complete than I would have wanted".

THE GIANT'S STONE (No.11)
Parish of Bisley-with-Lypiatt
SO 91770611

Potential visitors to this site might be forgiven for thinking this site is a standing stone, by examining the Ordnance Survey map. The **Transactions of the Bristol and Gloucestershire Archaeological Society** of 1960 lists this site as the Giant's Stone long barrow. No mound exists today. Crawford mentions this site:

"The barrow had been removed, or nearly so, leaving some of the stones which formed the chambers, especially a large one locally known as 'The Giant's Stone'".

When visited in December 1920 Crawford recorded two vertical moss-grown slabs spaced about six inches apart, placed parallel to eac other, the tops of which were about two feet above the ground. The long axes were due east and west. Roger Cudby and I made a thorough search of the area in the summer of 1986 and could find nothing. Our investigations led us to the 'Stirrup Cup' public house in Bisley where we were spun a tale by a local whose grandfather had farmed the land on which the barrow stood. The stones were carted away (he said) and one of them was left beside a field entry further up the lane to prevent carts from damaging the drystone wall. Sure enough a large stone can be seen by the side of the track. It is a long stone lying on its side and is about five to six feet long. Is this the Giant's Stone? Local historian Ronald Fletcher of Eastcombe thinks not. It is, he says, a stone from a now demolished barn. A similar stone can be found on the other side of the valley.

The original site was located eventually, but it is heavily overgrown. The long barrow was almost destroyed in 1883. Only the two stones, mentioned by Crawford, remained. It is just possible to see what may be the broken remains of one of the slabs buried in the ground. The fragments are totally invisible from the track, six feet away. Many visitors wander down Hayedge Lane in search of this 'stone'. They do not find it. Be warned.

HANGMAN'S STONE (No.12)
Parish of Hampnett
SP 08761512

This site, which consists of two stones, marks the junction of the parishes of Hampnett, Yarnworth and Stowell and might therefore indicate that the stone or stones were chosen to mark a boundary, that is assuming their antiquity. Crawford visited the site in 1920, but found nothing. He was later informed that the stone in question was one used as a stile. It obtained its name, apparently, from an incident involving a sheep rustler who, when getting over the stile with his spoils fell and was hung by the entangled sheep. However there are two stones at the site, one of which is a flat slab 4ins (0.1m) thick, 2ft8ins (0.81m) high and 2ft8ins (0.81m) wide. It is set into the drystone wall as a stile in a manner found elsewhere in the area. This is probably the stone mentioned by Crawford. The second stone, 7ft (2.13m) away, lies against the wall. It is an irregularly shaped slab, 7ft (2.13m) long and a maximum of 3ft (0.91m) high. It has an ovoid hole in the south end. It is possible that this stone may have once marked a gibbet, giving a more plausible reason for its name.

HANGMAN'S STONE (No.13)
On the boundary of the parishes of Siddington and Preston Lost. SU 0498979 (site of)

Crawford quotes Samuel Rudder's **History of Gloucestershire**, 1779:

"This parish (Preston-Ed.) is bounded to the westward by the Irmin-Street, one of the Roman ways passing through Cirencester; and at the distance of two miles from the town, but in this parish, there stands an antient rude stone, about 4 feet high, lately painted and mark'd as a milestone. This is vulgarly called 'Hangman's Stone' because, it is said, a fellow resting a sheep thereon (which he had stolen and tied its legs together for the convenience of carrying it) was there strangled, by the animal's getting its leggs round his neck in struggling".

A search was made recently but no trace of the stone could be found. It probably disappeared during road widening in 1966.

THE HOAR STONE (No.14)
Parish of Duntisbourne Abbots
SO 96490659

This stone stands at the east end of a ruined long barrow, 120ft (36.58m) long by 90ft (27.43m) wide and 3ft (0.9m) high. To the south of the centre of the barrow lies a large prostrate slab which is probably the capstone of the original chamber. Excavations in 1806 revealed the remains of eight or nine skeletons. The Hoar Stone (or Flight Stone) itself is a large lozenge shaped, weathered sarsen. Crawford quotes a source:

"The largest stone at the east end has long been known by the name of the 'Hoar Stone'; it is of the calcereous kind, 12 feet high, 13 feet in circumference and weighs between five and six tons; it was half above and half underground".

The barrow, now overgrown, lies in the middle of a cultivated field and is just visible from the road. Crawford visited the site in 1920. He noted that the eastern stone was not more than four feet above the surface of the mound which was low and much spread. This is much the state of things today.

19

THE HOAR STONE (No.15)
Parish of Lower Swell
SP 17022489

This megalith sits in the middle of a ploughed field about half a mile south-south-west of Lower Swell church. It consists of local oolite stone. There is no sign of a mound. It measures 5ft 7ins (1.7m) long by 3ft (0.9m) high by 2ft 3ins (0.7m) deep. Crawford quotes the gardener at Lower Swell Vicarage,

"...they tried to move it and found it eight feet deep in the ground, and the tackle broke as they were making the attempt."

We are fortunate that it did. However, another standing stone in Swell was not so lucky.

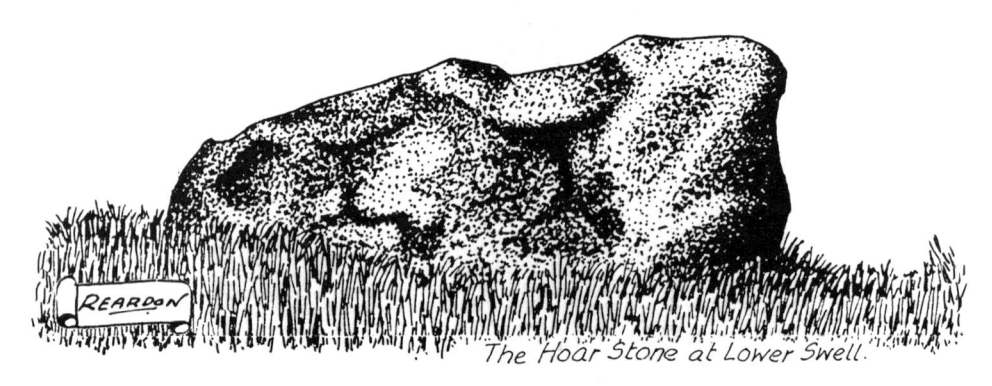

The Hoar Stone at Lower Swell

THE HORESTONE (No.16)
Rodborough Common

This stone, once used as a milestone, stands by the side of the road linking Rodbourough Common with Minchinhampton Common. It stands about five feet (1.52m) high and has a flat face facing the road and a curved back. The stone has been well worked in the past. There are many milestones and markstones on both commons and all around the Stroud valleys. These numerous stones are well documented in **Milestones of the Stroud District**, by Christopher Cox, from the **Transactions of the Bristol and Gloucestershire Archaeological Society**. In particular, Cox mentions stones 29 and 30 (by his numbering system) which are the Horestone and a similarly shaped stone a mile or so along the road on Minchinhampton Common. He says,

"Both these stones had a road plate, but are quite different in type from the others on this route". Both are tall, round headed pillars, the back rounded, the face flattened: the base of No.30 (and possibly No.29, though this standing less high probably has its base hidden in the turf) projects in front as a square step. The back of No.30 is deeply pitted with holes 1 inch in diameter approximately 1 inch apart". He goes on, "On the old abandoned track across Rodborough Common stand two stones, one 13ins x 5ins x 24ins, the other by its side, 14ins x 7ins x 48ins, the latter marked by various holes, some apparently apt to receive bars or bolts. The top of the taller stone has been broken diagonally. It seems possible that these stones, and Nos.29 and 30 may have originally been route markers over the Commons, and that the Cirencester plates were fixed to 28, 29 and 30 insitu: early maps give a numbered series from Cirencester to only No.31 by Minchinhampton. This, however, is conjecture".

Ronald Fletcher of Eastcombe has provided me with information which may confirm that the Horestone is certainly older than the other milestones in the district. It was probably adopted as a milestone due to its fortuitous position, as were many old stones. In the **Transactions of the Bristol and Gloucestershire Archaeologlical Society,** 1932 there is an article on the Minchinhampton Custumal, a detailed list of landowners and their estates and holdings, dating from the Middle Ages. Item 78 goes as follows, "Thomas atte Horstone for half a virgate and an assart at La Horstone". The footnote to the text is worth repeating.

"The Scandinavian 'Horgr' means 'sacred'. A Hoarstone crests a tumulus near Cirencester (Hoarstone barrow at Duntisbourne Abbots-Ed.) and there is a little Hoar Stone near Bisley. The word is often applied to boundary stones. Harridge, between Hereford and Worcester counties, was Hore rugge in 1275. The ancient boundary stone between Rodborough and Hampton not far from the 'Bear' Inn is much more ancient than the date upon it and was possibly one of the points on the boundary of the old three cassate estate of Woodchester".

It is clear that this stone is far older than the other associated milestones on the route and the derivation of its name suggests that it might be even older than the medieval reference.

IDEL BARROW (No.17)
Parish of Upton St Leonards

Crawford quotes, in Pope's Wood...

"it lies close to the ancient Portway, but I have not had an opportunity of examining the mound with the care necessary to say anything definite on the subject".

Crawford visited the site on December 17, 1920. The site lies at the junction of the parishes of Cranham, Painswick and Upton St Leonards. There was no trace of a mound. Mr St Clair Baddeley told Crawford that he had seen a large stone there, which might have been the last vestige of a chamber. There were boundary stones in the locality at one time, but had been lost by the time of Crawford's visit.

KIFTSGATE STONE (No.18)
Parish of Weston Subedge
SP 13513898

Another holed stone, 3ft (0.9m) high, like the High Cross stone at Elkstone, stands by the Cotswold Way and the road from Willersley to Mickleton. **Kifts** is thought to derive from Old English *cyft* meaning **meeting, conference,** hence Kiftsgate could mean **gate or gap where meetings are held.** And indeed the stone marks a former moot place where local people met to discuss tribal business, hold festivals and administer justice. Moot places were often sited at track crossings. Of course, the tracks may well have been formed after the stone was adopted. The word **gate** is derived from the Saxon **geat**, meaning a track. In the Domesday Book the area around the stone was called the Cheftsihat Hundred and meetings of the Kiftsgate hundred were held at the stone. It was the centre for local and national announcements including proclamations of the crowning of kings up to William IV.

KING CHARLES'STONE (No.19)
On the single track road between the B4073 Gloucester-Painswick road and the A4173 Gloucester-Stroud Road

A few yards down this lane from a stone folly, on the grass verge stands a small worked stone. It stands about three feet high. On its top is a brass stud or nail similar to those found on Ordnance Survey bench marks which suggests that it may have served such a purpose at one time. No other markings are visible on the stone. The Author was told, some years ago, that this stone was placed in this position by a group of people who believed that it had been removed from its original location in the past. Whether or not that is true the stone can be rocked to and fro. It is not bedded in the ground and this may substantiate the story. Older Ordnance survey maps show this stone as King Charles' Stone. The modern maps have no reference to it. A story is related in **Glimpses of the History of Painswick,** by F.A. Hyett.

"There is a story, dear to the heart of many a dweller in Painswick, which I feel constrained to treat as folklore rather than history. It rests solely on the authority of a passage in Rudder's **History of Gloucestershire** which I will quote. After mentioning the escarpment on the top of Painswick Hill, Rudder goes on to say: 'King Charles's army occupied this post after quitting the seige of Gloucester; and there is a tradition that the King, sitting on a stone near the camp, was asked by one of the young princes When should they go home? to which his majesty answered, a little disconsolately, that he had no home to go to'. If this event ever occurred it must have been on the evening of September 5 1643. A stone at the end of Seven Leaze Lane, on which Charles is supposed to have been sitting when he answered his son's question, has been marked on the Ordnance Map as 'King Charles's Stone', but the story appears to me intrinsically improbable".

LITTERIDGE CROSS (No.20)
Parish of Bisley-with-Lyppiat
SO 912056

In tithe documents the Litteridge Cross is mentioned as a notable landmark, but there is no evidence that it was a wayside cross. It has been suggested that it could have been a merestone with an incised cross. The stone is now lost although an incised cross was found at the Nelson Inn at Oakridge which may have been this cross. A square enclosure at the map reference is marked 'Litteridge Cross Piece' on the Bisley tithe map and a small field beside it, 'Against Litteridge Cross'. A large rock is shown close to a meeting of footpaths nearby (SO 91440550), but there is insufficient evidence to show that this is the stone in question.

LANG STONE (No.21)
Parish of Minchinhampton
Lost. SO 877007 (site of)

This stone, now lost, stood on the far side of the Bulwarks earthwork on Minchinhampton Common. Tradition states that it stood with two other stones (lost before Lang Stone was removed). All three were supposed to have marked the spot where three Danish chieftains were killed. There is a hollow to the south called Woeful Dane Bottom. Neither the stones nor the hollow have any connection with the Danes. Crawford concludes that the stones were probably the remains of a long barrow. We shall never know. Two large fragments of stone lie near Tom Long's Post, not far from this site. Could these be part of the remains of these lost megaliths?

24

THE LONG STONE (No.22)
Parish of Minchinhampton
ST 88369991

Perhaps the most famous Gloucestershire megalith, this stone stands in Hampton Fields, in the corner of a field, close by the road between Avening and Minchinhampton. There are, in fact, two stones, an oolite 'holey stone', upright 7ft9ins (2.36m) high and 18ins (0.46m) thick and a second stone 3ft2ins (0.97m) high, across which a drystone wall has been built. The two stones are 34ft (10.36m) apart and are believed to be in their original positions. It is thought by some that the stones are the last vestige of a long barrow. Samuel Rudder, (1799), likens the barrow on which the Long Stone stands to that of the Tingle Stone (No.38). No traces of a mound remain today. Three legends are attached to the larger of the pair. In the past mothers were wont to pass their rickety children through the hole in the stone in the belief that they would be cured of the condition. Other sources claim such passage as a cure for smallpox.

There are a great many traditions relating to the use of stones for healing purposes. These traditions can be found all over Europe. It is interesting to note that edicts were passed between AD450-1100, mostly in France and Spain, prohibiting visits to stones for the cure of disease. The prevention and cure of a variety of rheumatic illnesses could be obtained by crawling through the holed stone of the Men-an-tol group in West Penwith in Cornwall. Probably the most well known legend of the healing properties of stones is that recounted by Geoffery of Monmouth in his **History of the Kings of Britain**. He cites that certain megaliths (attributed by translators to Stonehenge) were of "medicinal virtue" and that by washing the stones and placing the sick in the water their illnesses would invariably be cured.

It has been suggested by dowsers and water diviners that standing stones were erected to mark the crossing point of two or more underground streams. Such subterranean confluences are referred to as 'blind springs'. Other dowsers have claimed to have detected other lines of influence at these places and have linked them with some form of force or earth energy. It has been suggested that such telluric forces manifest themselves at special points on the earth's surface in the form of spirals. It has been further suggested that these energies are somehow amplified by the insertion of a "needle of stone" above the energy point on the ground. Dowsable forces are said to be detectable on the surface of the stone and that they spiral up and down the stone in a cyclic pattern. The stone becomes 'charged', in a dowsing sense. Some dowsers have found that these charges do not remain static and that they may change from hour to hour. Others have shorter cyclic periods of change. Such 'energies' can be measured. Geomagnetic variations in standing stones can sometimes be measured using a simple hand held compass. Anomalies of a similar nature have been measured at the Long Stone and an account is given below.

All of this brings us to the other two legends associated with the Long Stone. It is said that when it hears the clock strike twelve the stone runs around the field. Another story tells of how the Long Stone goes down to the spring at Minchinhampton to drink. There are many traditions and stories that describe standing stones which turn in their holes and others that move at specific times. This may have its explanation in the kind of dowsing reaction experienced by Professor T C Lethbridge at the Merry Maidens stone circle in Cornwall. He was dowsing using a pendulum with his free hand placed on one of the stones.

"As soon as the pendulum started to swing, a strange thing happened. The hand resting on the stone received a strong tingling sensation like a mild electric shock and the pendulum itself shot out until it was circling nearly horizontally to the ground. The stone itself, which must have weighed over a ton, felt as though it were rocking and almost dancing about."

The spiralling energy pattern described previously shows up on the surface of the stone in bands which are detectable by dowsing. The dowser Tom Graves has described how these bands can produce some interesting side effects when a dowser or a particularly sensitive person comes into contact with them. This may be the original basis behind the belief of the power believed to be in stones. For instance, when a dowser leans against one of these bands on a standing stone it somehow affects his balance, producing an effect which feels like a slow and gentle push to one side or the other. This reaction may be the reason why another Gloucestershire stone(now lost) was called the Twizzlestone. Another effect of this band on a dowser can be quite violent. Less sensitive people can detect it as a warmth or tingle and this may be the reason why another Gloucestershire stone, not far from the Long Stone is known as the Tinglestone.

If this all sounds a little far fetched consider the following. Dowser Alan Lovejoy, in 1988, whilst attending a practical dowsing course, held in Stroud, by the British Society of Dowsers, made a brief trip, with some other delegates, to the Long Stone in order to dowse for energy lines. Quoting from Mr Lovejoy's article in **Gloucestershire Earth Mysteries**, No.7:

"I took my geomagnetometer with me and, what began as a casual experiment caused a major distraction amongst the twenty or so delegates, who included several engineers, a physicist and other professionals. As we left our cars and approached the Long Stone the geomagnetometer gave fairly high fluctuating readings; higher than average readings I had experienced back at the Stroud conference centre, earlier that day.

"As I got to the Long Stone the ground in the immediate vicinity was indicating between 5 and 7 on a scale of 10. Readings from the Long Stone itself took the needle completely across the scale, past 10 in a band approximately one foot deep and some 18ins from the ground. The instrument indicated zero on the rest of the stone, but may well have given a reading had I recalibrated it. These readings were carefully observed by a number of my course colleagues. By then virtually everyone was touching the stone and dowsing it and the surrounding area with dowsing rods and pendulum.

"Some ten minutes later we went back to take further readings at the Long Stone. Unexpectedly the readings showed zero. The 'band' had disappeared. This change in the level of readings immediately attracted attention. The concensus of opinion was that the presence of a score or more dowsers around the stone and interfering with the energy lines had caused a discharge from the stone!

"Immediately several members present suggested an experiment to 'recharge' the stone by the laying-on of hands on the stone. This happened with some half dozen people participating. After several minutes of this (whilst my geomagnetometer and I were under close scrutiny) the needle began to creep up from its zero position. This time the instrument detector head was taking the only detectable readings which came from the inside lower edge of the hole in the base of the stone near its centre. Within five minutes or so the reading reached 4.5, and with several of the 'chargers' complaining of headache and fatigue we ended the experiment.

"We carried on dowsing the site for a further half hour, and then before leaving returned to both stones. The final readings indicated that the Long Stone hole, centre side, was giving approximately 7."

It is apparent that the stone somehow interferes with the local geomagnetic field and that that interference is fluctuating. Furthermore the interaction of people around the stone appears to influence those fluctuations. Perhaps here is a clue to one of the original functions of the stone.

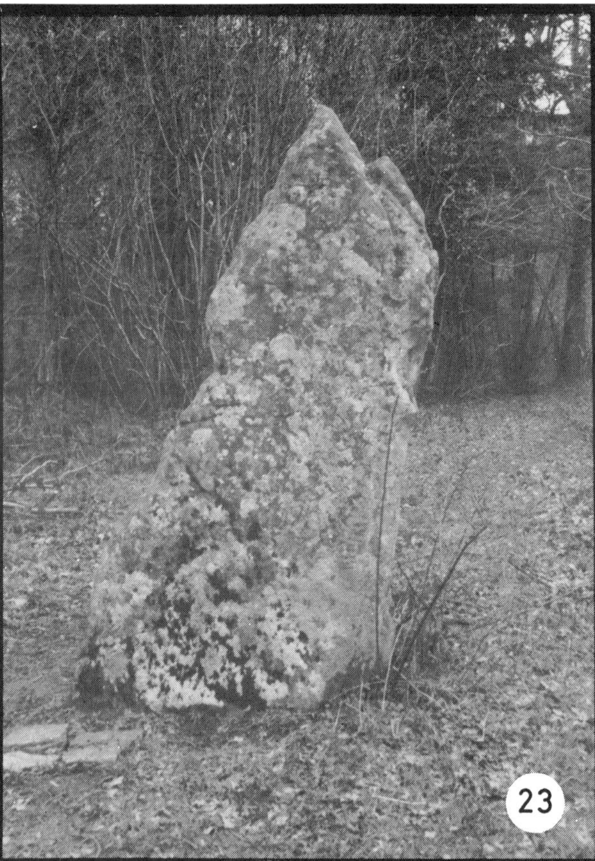

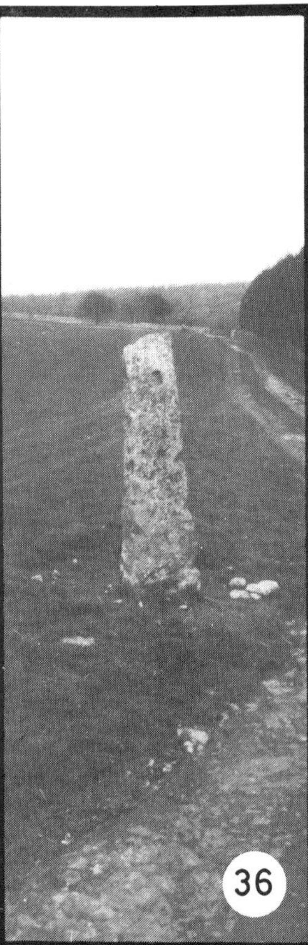

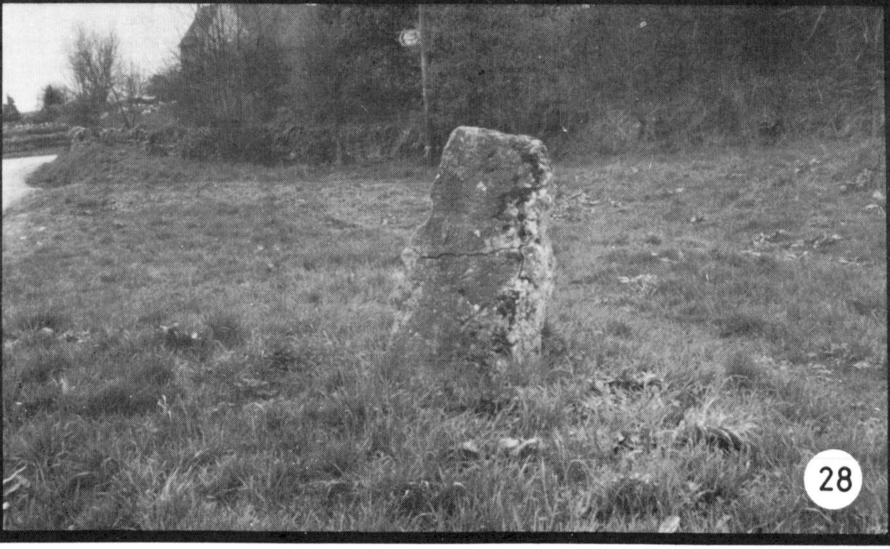

THE LONG STONE (No.23)
Parish of Staunton
SO 55931205

This monolith, of Old Red Conglomerate, stands by the side of the Gloucester to Monmouth road, about a mile from Coleford in the Forest of Dean. A note from Mr J.G. Wood (**Transactions of the Bristol and Gloucestershire Archaeological Society** vi.,1881-2,357), quoted by Crawford, says,

"The first halting place was at a remarkable monolith by the side of the highway.... This monolith is of unhewn stone, and stands 8ft above the ground, and probably it is as deep beneath it. It is known as the 'Long Stone'. No tradition concerning it remains except that if it be pricked by a pin exactly at midnight, it will bleed".

There are no visible traces of an associated mound or any other stones in the vicinity. Ray Wright quotes a source from 1857 telling of the carving of a mask on the side of the stone facing the road. I have been unable to find this piece of Victorian vandalism, but have, by photographic accident, noticed a bizarre simulacrum on the side of the stone facing towards Staunton. In the right conditions it is possible to discern the image of a human form, on the surface of the stone, with arms outstretched in the manner of a crucifixion.

The Long Stone forms the important centre point of Ray Wright's 'Leyline Cross', as described in **Secret Forest**. He describes the present height of the stone as 6ft. It may well have suffered damage in the past. As other megaliths in the locality have been destroyed completely we are fortunate that the Long Stone is still with us.

LONGSTONE (No.24)
Parish of English Bicknor
SO 562158

Crawford again quotes Wood:

"Of an entirely different class (from erratic blocks) is the 'Longstone' above Symonds Yat Station marked on Gloucestershire 30 NE. This is a natural stack or pillar left by the denudation of the Carboniferous Limestone cliff of which it is a portion. It is exactly analogous (in relationship to the outcrop and otherwise) to the Devil's Pulpit on the line of the Dyke on the cliff above the Plum weir at Tintern. This stack is called Longa Petra on the Dean Forest Survey of 1282."

In the cliffs adjacent to the Longstone has been found

evidence of human occupation going back to pre-Neolithic times (i.e. before 3000BC).

LONGSTONE, CLOSE TURF FARM (No.25)
Parish of St Briavel's
Lost. SO 581051 (site of)

This huge stone was destroyed over one hundred years ago. No trace of it remains today.

"'Longstone' was a sandstone of the district and stood out in the middle of a large field by itself, without mound or other stone near. It was not on the highest ground of its neighbourhood..." (1)

The field in which it stood is still called 'Longstone Field'. A portion of the stone can still be seen at the well at Close Turf Farm (SO 585048) where it is used as a water bucket stand.

"In March 1875, when visiting the antiquities of the Forest of Dean, I was in search of the 'Longstone', a monolith described by Samuel Rudder in his **History of Gloucestershire**, 1779, as 'a stone set on end...ten feet above the surface, six feet broad, and five feet thick'. Its situation is marked on the Ordnance Map (old one-inch engraved edition of 1830, Sheet 35) at about one and a half miles east of St Briavel's Castle; but as the roads are deep and winding, I had some trouble to find its exact location. On enquiring of a farm labourer for the 'Longstone' he replied with a broad grin, 'You be come too late, Sir,' and he then told me that the tenant farmer who had just entered on the farm on which the 'Longstone' had stood, had blown it to pieces with three charges of gunpowder, broken it up with sledges, and carted it into a quarry at the side of the field. The owner of the property was residing abroad. I visited the spot on which 'Longstone' had stood, and also the fragments, and was forcibly impressed with the need of some law to protect our national antiquities from wanton destruction". (2)

(1) and (2) from the **Proceedings of the Society of Antiquaries**, 2 S., vi., 1876, pp502-3.

TOM LONG'S POST (No.26)
Parish of Minchinhampton
SO 85890129

The lonely meeting place of five roads on the top of Minchinhampton Common, is reputed to be the burial place of suicide Tom Long. The site is now marked by a road sign bearing the name 'Tom Long's Post'. The place is also believed to heve been a gallows site in the post Medieval period. Adjacent to the sign post is a small stone standing about three feet (0.91m) high. A smaller stone of the same type lies a few yards away by the side of the road leading down to Burleigh and Brimscombe. Both may be remnants of other, now destroyed standing stones or long barrows. Both the Cobstone and Lang Stone stood near this spot.

LORD'S STONE (No.27)
Parish of Bisley

By the side of the road between Bisley and Stroud, near Stancomb Farm stands a base and a shaft of stone now guarded by iron railings and much overgrown. Miss Rudge's **History of Bisley** contains an interesting account of this stone. She says thet it once marked the boundary between the manors of Bisley and Lypiatt. The stone was, for centuries, known as the 'Lord's Stone' and it is mentioned in the Lypiatt MS book under the date 1654. She says that there is no doubt that the stone has always stood as the boundary mark between the two manors, and it was significant that its most richly carved front faced towards Bisley. The restorers of the stone and the builders of the railings re-erected the stone facing the wrong way so that its ancient significance is now lost.

Despite the above other sources tell me that the stone once stood at Stancombe crossroads and was removed and re-erected in its present location, further along the road, by the local landowner, because it was in danger of being damaged by farm carts.

On the front face of the stone is the figure of a saint with uplifted arms standing beneath a round arch. There are six holes on the left which were probably the plug holes for an iron plate, as the stone was used for a milestone in later times, and as an indication of the limits of the Bisley parish in that direction. The south side of the stone also has the figure of a saint, probably the Blessed Virgin Mary, under a round arch. Miss Rudge:

"If the Lord's Stone has always been so called we probably have in it the original indication of the division of the Manor of Bisley in Norman times. At the same time it must be stated that experts have suggested the possibility of its being of Saxon or even Roman origin".

MARKSTONE (No.28)
Eastleach Martin

This three feet high, unworked mark stone stands on the edge of a green adjacent to the River Leach in the village of Eastleach Martin. A local resident told me that the stone was set up to mark the old route to the nearby old stone footbridge, Keble's Bridge, which connects the village to its sister Eastlech Turville. About a hundred yards along the road from the green stands a dressed stone wellhead covering a gushing spring. Another small stone can be seen built into the churchyard wall across the river at Eastleach Turville.

On a recent visit to photograph this stone I was saddened to see that it had been severely damaged. The stone has been struck by a very heavy object, probably an earth moving vehicle (there are some recent works on the other side of the road) and is cracked right through.

ODO AND DODO (No.29)
Parish of Gotherington
SO 9828 and 9829 (original locations)

These two uprights were standing in Nottingham Hill hillfort until about 1860. When Crawford published **Long Barrows of the Cotswolds** the stones had been removed to the grounds of Prescott House. One stood about 7ft (2.13m) high and the other a foot shorter. Both tapered to a rough point. I would be pleased to hear if these stones or their remains are still in existence. Oddo and Doddo were founders of Tewkesbury Abbey (AD 1102). One presumes the stones are not their petrified remains.

38

Lord's Stone
In the Parish of Bisley. 27 PTR

37

OUDUCEUS'S STONE (No.30)
Parish of Tidenham
ST 531947 (site of Striguil Bridge)

Crawford quotes Mr J.G. Wood:

"At the Roman bridge-crossing there was formally a stone 6 feet by four feet (about) and how deep I cannot say, as it was sunk in the alluvium all but about 3 feet. Perhaps it should be called a pair of stones; for it was sharply and cleanly divided into two equal halves. It lay close to the edge of high water. It is clearly the stone of which a story is told of Bishop Ouduceus in 'Liber Landavensis' (1893). That is, that, to show his miraculous powers to Gildas, he took an axe and split the stone. This (like the others) was of Old Red Conglomerate. When I last went to look for them they had disappeared - sunk, I suppose into the alluvium, for the bank had been a good deal denuded".

The stone and the bridge are both now gone.

PATTEN STONE (No.31)
Parish of Ruspidge
SO 65640959

Stone hunters will note that the site of this stone, ten yards west of the Dean road, is marked on the current Ordnance Survey maps for the Forest of Dean. However it no longer remains, having been taken in 1922 to make a culvert under the Crown road. A.W. Trotter, in **The Dean Road**, 1936, suggests that the name implied that the Patten Stone was the base of a column. He was told by a local that it bore "writing in a foreign language". It has been suggested elsewhere that it was a Roman milestone. Other informants recall that it bore the design of a patten or a shoe.

Ray Wright, in **Secret Forest**, mentions a stone just north of Blackpool Bridge, close to the Parkend to Blakeney Road. This is a mass of Devonian Conglomerate, known locally as the 'Drummer Boy Stone'. It measures 5ft (1.5m) x3ft 3ins (1m) with about an inch (25mm) protruding above ground level. Wright suggests that its name may have derived from a drummer boy who was killed in the area and buried by or near this stone. Alternatively he suggests that **boy** could derive from the Old Norman word **boyau**, which means **bowl**; the shape of the depressions on the top surface of the stone. The Drummer Boy Stone could be the Patten stone, moved during the road repairs in 1922. Its location at SO 656091 is very close to the site of the Patten Stone.

34

PEAKED STONE (No.32)
Parish of Horsley
Lost. SO 85509764(site of)

Crawford notes that this, now lost monolith, was removed at around the time of the demise of the Cobstone. The Peaked or Picked Stone is shown on the 1-inch Ordnance Survey map of 1828 where there is a rise in the ground. It was not concluded as being part of a long barrow. The monolith stood about 4ft (1.22) high and was removed by 1868 and used to build steps in a farm yard near Barton End. The original site of the stone is close to a triangulation point shown on the modern Ordnance Survey map.

I recently visited this site with local historian Ronald Fletcher, taking the old coach road from Nailsworth which runs up and alongside the triangular field where the Peaked Stone once stood. He assured me that the stone was still standing in the field when he was a boy, over fifty years ago, and that he can remember it being removed to the side of the field. There are many fragments of stone lying in the hedges on both sides of the field which are probably field clearance stone. The original site is on the highest point in the area. There is no sign of a triangulation pillar but a small oval area about twelve feet long by seven feet wide has been avoided by the plough, the centre of which is a small heap of broken stones. Could this mark the site of the now lost Peaked Stone?

THE SPEECH STONE (No.33)
Speech House, near Cinderford
SO 619122

Opposite the main entrance to the Speech House, on the side of the road, stands a stone pillar which traditionally marks the centre of the Forest of Dean. It lay in the undergrowth for many years, but has been restored to its original position. The stone is modern, but may mark the site of an older monolith Alfred Watkins, in **The Old Straight Track** mentions a ley which runs from the stone at Speech House down to the Hermitage at Courtfield on the other side of the River Wye at Lower Lydbrook.

STANDING STONES (No.34)
Parish of Kingscote
ST 81189467

This site consists of a number of stones mentioned in the Archaeological Record. An upright has been built into the north side of a field wall, its upper end being free. It is about 3ft 3ins (1m) high, 1ft 6ins (0.45m) wide and 1ft 6ins (0.45m) thick. South of the wall lies a larger stone 4ft 7ins (1.4m) long and 3ft 3ins (1m) wide, partly buried in the ground. Two other very large stones are built into the north side of the wall a little further along from the upright. Several other stones, all larger than one might expect for wall building, can be seen in the wall. These may be the remnants of a chamber from a long barrow. I have yet to visit this site which lies some distance from a footpath or road.

STONE ON SELSLEY COMMON (No. 35)

A stone can be seen in the garden of a house on Selseley Common, next to the road to Dursley, close to the edge of the common. It is a flat, roughly triangular shaped slab standing about three to four feet high (0.9-1.2m). It is surrounded by a ring of concrete bollards. It looks very much as if it has been re-erected as a garden feature. Its shape suggests that it might be a stone from one of the many nearby long barrows, denuded and robbed of its stone in past centuries.

OLD STONE GATEPOST (No. 36)
Parish of Bourton-on-the-Hill
SP 14413195

Traditionally known as 'the Roman stone' this monument stands on one of the highest points of Bourton Downs not far from the course of Ryknild Street, hence its name. It is, however, probably of post-medieval date and, furthermore, a gatepost. But at 5ft 8ins (1.73m) in height it must have held a very tall gate. It is of hewn limestone with four, smooth, tapering faces and rectangular in section. The top is broken off. There are two chiselled bolt holes on the south face and there is damage on the corners suggesting that farm implements may have been sharpened on it. The adjacent field is the site of a Saxon Burial place and a slight mound and outcrop of stone can be seen from this site

The stone lies on a track about fifty yards from the public footpath that runs past Bourton Hill House from the turning off the A424.

THE TIBBLESTONE (No. 37)
Parish of Teddington
SO 96333383

The Tibblestone is a holed, roughly cylindrical, monolith about 4ft (1.2m) in height which stands on the Cheltenham side of the Teddington Cross Hands road junction on the A453/A438. There is a legend that a giant who lived on Dixton Hill (midway between Gotherington and Gretton) would amuse himself by throwing rocks at ships sailing up the Severn past Tewkesbury. This would have been quite some feat as the Severn is, at its closest to Dixton Hill, seven miles away. Nevertheless during one fusillade the giant slipped and fell. The mark where he fell can still be seen on the side of the hill which is crowned with earthworks. The stone which he had been throwing fell short of its intended target (and well off it if you look at the map) and landed somewhere near the Cross Hands at Teddington. The stone remained hidden for many years, the legend being a folk memory of its existence. In 1948 Mr C.J. Lucy of the Teddington garage found what was thought to have been the stone whilst excavating for foundations. It was clearly a worked stone and Mr Lucy called in expert help. It was concluded that this must have been the Tibblestone, which was marked on ancient maps of the area. The stone was re-erected by the side of the old road. Since then the road has been redirected a short distance north and a roundabout constructed. It is not clear whether the stone was erected where it was found or where it was believed to have stood.

Checks have been made for an alignment linking Dixton Hill and the Tibblestone. Two possible alignments show up on the map; one links the old crossroads at Teddington Hands with Dixton Hill earthworks and Belas Knap long barrow. The other links the first two sites with another old stone near Northleach called the Hangman's Stone. Fieldwork might reveal a clincher point on either of these alignments, but without accurate knowledge of the original location of the Tibblestone such suggestions can only be speculative.

The Tibblestone was used as a boundary marker at one time. It marked the extent of the Tibblestone Hundred, which might indicate that the stone predated the boundary thus confirming its antiquity and legitimacy as a ley mark stone. A similar story is attached to another standing stone - the Broadstone, at Stroat (No.1).

THE TINGLESTONE (No.38)
Parish of Avening
ST 88239899

This stone, 6ft (1.83m) high, stands at the high end of a Neolithic long barrow named after the megalith. This long barrow, 130ft (39.6m) long, lies just off Step's Lane which runs through Gatcombe Park. Although the lane is a public right of way the field in which the Tinglestone stands is not. As Gatcombe Park is in Royal ownership the area is constantly patrolled by security officers and public access to the site is restricted. The long barrow, however, is in the field where the annual horse trials are held and access to the stone might be possible on those days. It is not advisable to attempt access without permission. The westerly post of a gateway, just north of the barrow, is of weathered oolite, four and a half feet high by two feet by one foot (1.37m x 0.6m x 0.3m), and may have come from the long barrow.

Crawford visited the site in 1920 when it was in the ownership of one Colonel Ricardo. He describes the Tinglestone as a slab of oolite very like the Long Stone. It stands on the north end of the barrow which is oriented north-south.

It has been suggested above that the name of this stone might be attributable to the tingling sensation sometimes felt at old stones. Indeed I, not prone to sensitivity of this sort, have experienced exactly that sensation whilst dowsing at the Tinglestone. This stone has also indicated magnetic anomalies. However, it is often easy to read too great a significance into a name. Another name for this stone was Tingwall Stone, which itself suggests another possible function for the monument. **Ting** is an Old Norse word meaning **assembly**. The tings or moot circles of the Orkneys were still in use as late as 1602, while the moot hill, Tynwald Hill, in the Isle of Man, is still in use today. The Tingwall Stone may well have marked an important meeting place in the distant past. This is a function which is associated with other Gloucestershire stones.

THREE MEGALITHS (No.39)
Parish of Beverstone
ST 85199537

Again from the Archaeological Record of 1950 there is mention of two possible megaliths in a ploughed field. One measures about 6ft by 4ft6ins (1.83m x 1.37m) with its upper surface level with the ground. The other is 6ft (1.83m) by 5ft6ins (1.68m) by 1ft6ins (0.46m) thick, partially buried with its end protruding from the ground. There are several large stones in the covert wall opposite. A survey, undertaken in 1973, notes three moss-covered recumbent stones then under the beginnings of a field clearance heap. Although there is no sign of a mound the location is typical for that of a long barrow. In 1977 a further slab 2ft 8ins(0.8m) by 1ft 8ins (0.5m) was noted in the south-east corner of the field. As with the site at Kingscote this site is well off the beaten track and I have yet to locate it.

TWIZZLE STONE (No.40)
Parish of Bisley-with-Lypiatt
SO 910053

The Archaeological Record contains a reference to this stone made by Crawford in 1925, who mentions its appearance on the 1873 Tithe Award Map for Bisley. No trace of this stone was found when the site was investigated in 1977. Does any trace of it remain today?

The extent of Bisley Common was at one time marked by mere stones. Some of these stones have since disappeared, but their locations have been preserved in field names such as Hoarstone and Twizzlestone. One of the surviving boundary stones can be seen by the left hand side of the road from Bisley to Oakridge.

The name of the Twizzle Stone, as inferred above, might be a folk memory of the geophysical dowsing effect mentioned in connection with the Tingle Stone. A more mundane origin for this name might well have been the local Twissel or Twyssell family of the parish.

WHITTLESTONE (No.41)
Parish of Lower Swell
Moved. Original location imprecise.
SP 17302534 (present site)

Crawford mentions that the site only of this stone was marked on the 1903 Ordnance Survey map. It was on the top of a ridge. There were no signs of a mound. Crawford quotes the Reverend David Royce,

"Within a stone's throw from the north-west angle of the church, on the summit of the rising ground, in the allotments, stood, within the memory of the writer of this paper, a familiar, yet most venerable monolith. It was known as the Whistlestone. This stone was the last, most probably, of a cist. Many bones were found at its base. A witticism amongst the villagers was this:-

'When the Whistlestone hears Stow clock (a mile off) strike twelve, it goes down to Lady Well (at the hill's foot) to drink'. Alas poor Whistlestone. Farmer Illes, one of the olden time, one day picked up two of a perfect set of teeth, in ploughing by the stone, but so harried was he by the wierdy teeth that he replaced them speedily where he found them. But a later occupier did what the good folk of the village declared could not be done-for 'all the King's horses and all the King's men' could not cast down nor carry away Whistlestone-but it was carried away-yet rescued from roads or profane use. In the vicarage paddock the prehistoric block now finds asylum".

The Whittlestone (to give it its current name) can be seen on the verge by the side of the road leading up towards the church and Upper Swell. It is now a round pudding shaped mass about 18ins (0,46m) thick and has a plaque attached with the following inscription:

"This ancient stone originally sited about 200 yards from the north-west corner of the church is a relic of the Neolithic age c.2000 BC associated presumably with the mode of human burial practised at that period."

Whilst every care has been taken to ensure the accuracy of the information contained in this book, neither the author nor publishers hold themselves responsible for any errors that may be found, or for the readers' interpretation of text or illustrations.

BIBLIOGRAPHY

Bord, J and C
The Secret Country
Granada Publishing Ltd.
1978
Crawford, O.G.S.
Long Barrows of the Cotswolds
John Bellows
1925
Devereux, Paul
Places of Power
Blandford
1990
Graves, Tom
Needles of Stone
Turnstone Press Ltd.
1978
Hadingham, Evan
Circles and Standing Stones
Heinmann
1975
Hitching, Francis
Earth Magic
Cassell and Co.Ltd
1976
Hoskins, W.G.
The Making of the English Landscape
Hodder and Stoughton
1955
Lethbridge, T.C.
The Legend of the Sons of God
Routledge and Keegan Paul
1972
Michell, John
The Old Stones of Landsend
Garnstone Press
1974
Robins, Don
Circles of Silence
Souvenir Press Ltd.
1985
Sullivan, D.P. (Ed.)
Gloucestershire Earth Mysteries, Various Editions
Gloucestershire Earth Mysteries
1985-90
Underwood, Guy
The Pattern of the Past
Museum Press
1969
Watkins, Alfred
The Old Straight Track
Methuen and Co.
1925

LIST OF SITES

1. THE BROADSTONE
Parish of Tidenham
ST 57769723

2. THE BUCKSTONE
Parish of Staunton
SO 54151230

3. BUTTINGTON TUMP
Parish of Tidenham
ST 54789306

4. BLACK HEDGE FARM STONE CIRCLES
Parish of Leckhampton

5. STONE AT CHALFORD
On the Chalford-Hyde-Minchinhampton road

6. THE COBSTONE
Parish of Minchinhampton
Lost. ST856000 or ST 877899 (site of)

7. THE DEVIL'S CHURCHYARD
Parish of Minchinhampton
SO 899003

8. DURSLEY MERE STONE
On the boundary of the parishes of Dursley and Cam
ST 78579618

9. STONES AT ELKSTONE
Parishes of Elkstone and Cowley

10. GATTLES CROSS
Clearwell Meend, Sling
SO 583085

11. THE GIANT'S STONE
Parish of Bisley-with-Lypiatt
SO 91770611

12. HANGMAN'S STONE
Parish of Hampnett
SP 08761512

13. HANGMAN'S STONE
On the boundaries of the parishes of Siddington and Prestom
Lost. SU 0498979 (site of)

14. THE HOAR STONE
Parish of Duntisbourne Abbots
SO 96490659

15	THE HOAR STONE	

15 THE HOAR STONE
    Parish of Lower Swell
    SP 17022489

16 THE HORESTONE
    Rodborough Common

17 IDEL BARROW
    Parish of Upton St Leonards

18 KIFTSGATE STONE
    Parish of Weston Subedge
    SP 13513898

19 KING CHARLES'STONE
    On the single track road between the B4073
    Gloucester-Painswick road and the
    A4173 Gloucester-Stroud Road

20 LITTERIDGE CROSS
    Parish of Bisley-with -Lyppiat
    SO 912056

21 LANG STONE
    Parish of Minchinhampton
    Lost. SO 877007 (site of)

22 THE LONG STONE
    Parish of Minchinhampton
    ST 88369991

23 THE LONG STONE
    Parish of Staunton
    SO 55931205

24 LONGSTONE
    Parish of English Bicknor
    SO 562158

25 LONGSTONE, CLOSE TURF FARM
    Parish of St Briavel's
    Lost. SO 581051 (site of)

26 TOM LONG'S POST
    Parish of Minchinhampton
    SO 85890129

27 LORD'S STONE
    Parish of Bisley

28 MARKSTONE
    Eastleach Martin

29   ODO AND DODO
       Parish of Gotherington
       SO 9828 and 9829 (original locations)

30   OUDUCEUS'S STONE
       Parish of Tidenham
       ST 531947 (site of Striguil Bridge)

31   PATTEN STONE
       Parish of Ruspidge
       SO 65640959

32   PEAKED STONE
       Parish of Horsley
       Lost. SO 85509764(site of)

33   THE SPEECH STONE
       Speech House, near Cinderford
       SO 619122

34   STANDING STONES
       Parish of Kingscote
       ST 81189467

35   STONE ON SELSLEY COMMON

36   OLD STONE GATEPOST
       Parish of Bourton-on-the-Hill
       SP 14413195

37   THE TIBBLESTONE
       Parish of Teddington
       SO 96333383

38   THE TINGLESTONE
       Parish of Avening
       ST 88239899

39   THREE MEGALITHS
       Parish of Beverstone
       ST 85199537

40   TWIZZLE STONE
       Parish of Bisley-with-Lypiatt
       SO 910053

41   WHITTLESTONE
       Parish of Lower Swell
       Moved. Original location imprecise.
       SP 17302534 (present site)